To Mom, with love — T.R.

The editors would like to thank
BARBARA KIEFER, Ph.D.,
Charlotte S. Huck Professor of Children's Literature,
The Ohio State University,
for her assistance in the preparation of this book.
Technical review provided by the American Academy of Pediatrics.

Visit us on the Web!
www.randomhouse.com/kids
www.seussville.com

Educators and librarians, for a variety of teaching tools, visit us at
www.randomhouse.com/teachers

Library of Congress Cataloging-in-Publication Data
Rabe, Tish.
Oh the things you can do that are good for you! / by Tish Rabe ; illustrated by Aristides Ruiz.
  p. cm.
ISBN 978-0-375-81098-5 (trade) — ISBN 978-0-375-91098-2 (lib. bdg.)
1. Health—Juvenile literature. 2. Children—Health and hygiene—Juvenile literature.
[1. Health.] I. Ruiz, Aristides, ill. II. Title. III. Series.
RA777 .R33 2001 613—dc21 00-065320

Printed in the United States of America
32 31 30 29 28 27 26 25

Oh, the THINGS you can DO that are GOOD for You!

by Tish Rabe

illustrated by Aristides Ruiz

The Cat in the Hat's Learning Library®

Random House 🏠 New York

I'm the Cat in the Hat
and today is the day,
so jump in, buckle up—
we must leave right away

for the Feeling Great Clinic
in far-off Fadoo.
It's a place part museum,
part circus, part zoo,

where you soon will learn how
to take good care of you!
(Your mother will not
mind at all if you do.)

Feeling Great
CLINIC

Here we are—and the first
friends I'd like you to meet
are two of the famous
Tac-Toe-Tapping Tweet.

Tweet shoot beezerball baskets
by using their feet.

They play every day.
They are strong and they're wise,
for they know to stay healthy
they need exercise!

Exercise gives you energy
and helps you grow.
It gets your heart beating
and makes your blood flow.

What's the Snuff-Gruffle's trouble?
There's no time to play
'cause he sneezes at least
ninety times every day.

When you sneeze, you blow dust
in a rush from your nose.
(My Sneeze-Meter measures
how far the dust goes.)

It can travel five feet
and blasts out with great power,
at speeds over one hundred
miles an hour!

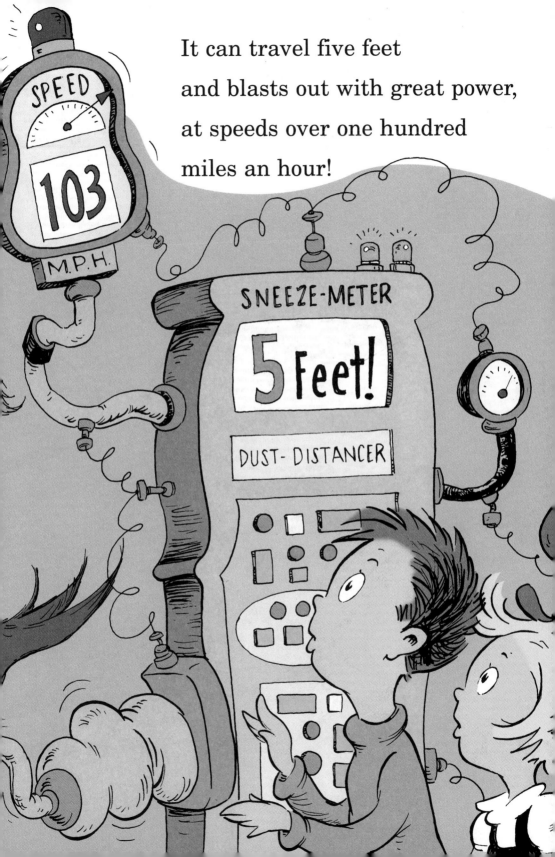

Sneezing shoots germs out
all over the place,
so lift up your arm
and cover your face.

Sneeze into your elbow
so friends won't get sick.

12

Or sneeze into a tissue—
and throw it out quick!

Germs are small living things
too tiny to see.
Most germs, it is true,
will not hurt you or me.

Now you're in for a treat—
meet the Zing-Singing Zanz.
She has written a song
about washing your hands!

It takes half a minute
to get your hands clean.
Sing along with the Zanz
and you'll see what I mean.

14

"Wishily washily washily wish.
Squishily squashily squashily squish.

Wash your hands carefully.
It's up to you.
Use soap and warm water.
It's easy to do.

16

Rinse them and while
we all sing this refrain,

germs from your hands
will slide right down the drain!"

To stay healthy, you need
to keep all of you clean.
So jump into my new
Scrubble-Bubble Machine.

It's part shower, part car wash
and costs just a dime.

It will give you shampoo
(either lemon or lime),
scrub your fingernails free
of the dirt and the grime,
while you finish your homework
at the same time!

Now please follow me—
you'll be glad that you did
as we tiptoe inside . . .

. . . the Great Food Pyramid!

Meet the Ee-hip-en-hop,

who are experts at knowing

what foods are the best

for a body that's growing.

They eat—

pasta, rice, cereal,

muffins, and breads,

which they munch at small tables

they wear on their heads.

Fruits, vegetables,
lean meats, and fish they enjoy
(although some prefer tofu
or milk made from soy).

They like all different foods
but are careful to eat
only morsels of fat
and few things that are sweet.

In the morning, your body
needs food right away.
So be sure to eat breakfast
to start off each day!

In this booth
you'll hear something amazing but true.
You will hear your own body—
it's talking to you!

When you're thirsty, just listen.
Your body says, "Think!
I need to get water—
please drink, drink, drink, drink!"

When you're hungry, your stomach
starts grumbling and mumbling,
"Feed me, or else
I will go right on rumbling!"

When your body feels pain,
it is telling you, "Hey!
Something is wrong.
I need help right away!"

If you start to feel tired,
you can't do your best.
Your body is telling you,
"It's time to rest."

If a voice inside says,
"I feel angry. I'm mad."
Or you hear your heart whisper,
"I feel kind of sad . . ."

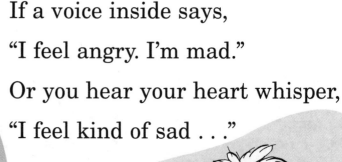

. . . tell a friend how you're feeling
and know it's okay.
Everyone at some time
gets to feeling that way.

Let me introduce
the Snee Snicker Sneeth!
She is known far and wide
for her sparkling, clean teeth.

Like you, she had baby teeth
when she was small,

but though she grew big,
her teeth grew not at all.

One by one they fell out,
but this smart Snicker Sneeth
knew she had a new set
of teeth growing beneath!

But there's one thing no Sneeth
you will meeth will forget—
this next set of teeth
is the last set you get.

So she brushes her teeth
at least two times a day.
(Germs that stay on your teeth
can lead to decay.)

After brushing your teeth,
take some floss and unwind it.
Then slide it between them.
If food's there—you'll find it!

Keep brushing and flossing—
it's really a breeze
and will help to make sure
you avoid cavities!

Now I'd like you to meet
the Galactic Garoo.
He can juggle six chairs,
five friends, and one shoe.

How do Garoo do it?
It's hard to explain,
but it all comes from signals
sent out from the brain.

It's your body's computer
that makes everything go.
Helps you sleep, run, and hiccup,
think, dream, smile, and grow.

It's important for you to
protect it, and so . . .

. . . if you're going out riding
a skateboard or bike,
or doing another fun sport
that you like,

take care to make sure
that your head is all right:
Grab a helmet, and see that
you snap it on tight!

Be smart and be safe,
and just like the Garoo,
make sure that your parents
wear their helmets, too!

Here is where Snug Buggles
tumble and play,
then sleep in a heap
at the end of the day.

Snug Buggles know
the importance of rest.
Ten hours of sleep
helps Buggles do best.

Snug Buggles show us
the way to wake bright—

Go to sleep at about
the same time every night.

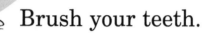

Brush your teeth.

Read a book.

Sing a song.

Dim the light.

Take a breath.
Close your eyes.
Just relax . . .

. . . and sleep tight.

We all need to sleep.
It's important to do.
But your brain never sleeps.
It keeps working for you.

It keeps your heart beating
inside of your chest
and keeps your lungs breathing
while you get some rest.

Oh, and speaking of sleep,
it is time we must go—
but there's just one more thing
I would like you to know.

You're important and special.
Believe me, it's true!
No one in the world
is exactly like you.

Feeling Great
CLINIC

We learned something together
in far-off Fadoo—
taking care of yourself
is a good thing to do.

GLOSSARY

Cavity: A hole in a tooth caused by decay.

Clinic: A place to get medical treatment.

Decay: To lose strength; to rot.

Energy: The ability to be active.

Exercise: Any activity that promotes physical fitness.

Pyramid: A figure having three or more triangular sides that meet in a point at the top.

Refrain: A part of a song or poem that is repeated.

Tofu: A soft, white food made from soybeans that is high in protein.

FOR FURTHER READING

The Berenstain Bears Go to the Doctor and *The Berenstain Bears Visit the Dentist* by Stan and Jan Berenstain (Random House, First Time Books®). Two helpful stories in which Brother and Sister Bear go for checkups. For preschoolers and up.

Dinosaurs Alive and Well! A Guide to Good Health by Laurie Krasny Brown and Marc Brown (Little, Brown). Dinosaurs advise young readers on topics such as diet, stress, and exercise. For kindergarten and up.

The Edible Pyramid: Good Eating Every Day by Loreen Leedy (Holiday House). The headwaiter at the Edible Pyramid Restaurant explains what foods belong in each part of the food pyramid and how many servings we should eat of each. For preschoolers and up.

Germs Make Me Sick! by Melvin Berger, illustrated by Marylin Hafner (HarperTrophy, Let's-Read-and-Find-Out Science®, Stage 2). All about the bacteria and viruses that make us sick. For kindergarten and up.

INDEX